The Four Keys to Defeating Accusations

Second Edition

Dismantle the Accusations That Are Destroying Your Life and Gain Peace and Victory!

By

Dr. Ron M. Horner

The Four Keys
to Defeating Accusations

Second Edition

Dismantle the Accusations That Are Destroying Your Life and Gain Peace and Victory!

By

Dr. Ron M. Horner

LifeSpring International Ministries
PO Box 5847
Pinehurst, North Carolina 28374
www.RonHorner.com

The Four Keys to Defeating Accusations – Second Edition

Dismantle the Accusations That Are Destroying Your Life and Gain Peace and Victory!

The Four Keys to Defeating Accusations taken from:

The Courts of Heaven: An Introduction

Copyright © 2024 Dr. Ron M. Horner

Scripture is taken from the New King James Version®. Copyright © 1982 by Thomas Nelson. Used by permission. All rights reserved. (Unless otherwise noted.)

Scripture quotations marked (GW) are taken from GOD'S WORD® Copyright© 1995 by God's Word to the Nations. All rights reserved.

Scripture marked (MIRROR) is taken from The Mirror Study Bible by Francois du Toit. Copyright © 2021 All Rights Reserved. Used by permission of The Author.

All rights reserved. This book is protected by the copyright laws of the United States of America. This book may not be copied or reprinted for commercial gain or profit. The use of short quotations or occasional page copying for personal or group study is permitted and encouraged. Permission will be granted upon request.

Trademarks are the property of their respective owners.

Requests for bulk sales discounts, editorial permissions, or other information should be addressed to:

LifeSpring Publishing
PO Box 5847
Pinehurst, NC 28374 USA

Additional copies available at www.ronhorner.com

TP ISBN: 978-1-953684-62-2
eBook: 978-1-953684-63-9

Cover Design by Darian Horner Design
(www.darianhorner.com)

Second Edition: December 2024

10 9 8 7 6 5 4 3 2 1 0

Printed in the United States of America.

Table of Contents

Acknowledgments i
Preface iii
Chapter 1 The Purpose of Accusations 1
Chapter 2 Accusations Reveal Strategy 23
Chapter 3 Dismantling the Accusations 27
Chapter 4 The Mercy Court QuickGuide 41
Chapter 5 Accusations Against Spiritual Sight 53
Chapter 6 The Weapon of Blue Capture Bags 57
Chapter 7 Conclusion 61
Description 63
About the Author 65
Other Books by Dr. Ron M. Horner 67
Personal Advocacy Sessions 71

Acknowledgments

Thanks to the wonderful team that works with LifeSpring to bring freedom to so many. Their work has eternal consequences. Lives have been changed, families restored, ministries and businesses brought into new places all because of the self-less servants of the King of kings. Thank you all.

Preface

Over the last few years, I have taught a significant amount on understanding the operations of the Courts of Heaven prayer paradigm. The responses I have received range from one extreme to the other. Many of the criticisms of the concept of a court system in Heaven appear to come from those who have not read their Bible with an open mind or have only read it with a mindset of protecting their pet belief system.

When I was first instructed to study the "Courts of Heaven," I began by identifying court-related terms in the Bible, such as petition, judge, court(s), witness, etc. Using my eSword® Bible Software program, I initially found over 1,700 verses that dealt with these terms in some way. Of course, not all of them were relevant, but upon further examination, an estimated eighty percent or more would have applied. That is a lot of scripture.

After studying the subject for several months, I realized that much more was said about the issue than I first realized, so with more research, the number of verses grew to over 3,500. I know of no subject with as many potential scripture references addressing the topic in some form. Even if less than half of those scriptures applied, we still look at a significant number. Can you name an item that has more scriptures?

We often forget that the first five books of our Old Testament are books of the Law—not merely religious law, but laws impacting the governance of all society. Many nations have modeled their systems of legislation on those found in the Bible. Laws are the guidelines by which court systems operate. We have a book in the Bible called Judges, which chronicles the leadership of the nation of Israel through men and women who governed and judged cases within the country. We have four books that chronicle the kings of Israel who often stood as judges over the nation and even have a record of judgments they pronounced. The book of Job starts in a courtroom in Heaven. The psalmist David decries his many defenses against his foes throughout the book of Psalms. His imprecatory prayers were cries for justice against those who opposed him. We have Daniel, who describes a courtroom scene in Heaven. We also read of Zechariah, who, in chapter 3, is found in a Court of Heaven, and Isaiah, who is instructed by the Lord to bring forth his case. The list could go on. To say that the concept of the Courts of Heaven cannot be found in the Bible is unfounded.

I have been involved in ministry since I was fourteen. I have attended a Bible college and seminary. I also have two doctoral degrees in ministry and quite a lot of study time under my belt. As a teacher by nature, I want a scriptural basis for what I am teaching, and I want it in context. By pulling scripture out of context, entire paradigms and belief systems can be developed to lead millions astray. If the Courts of Heaven is an important concept we need to understand, then we can find it in the Word of God.

In studying the Word of God, I realize that many important concepts are seemingly veiled from a general view until you begin to explore the idea. That is how parables work. You qualify yourself for the truth hidden in the parable by digging the truth out. Less than thirty miles from my home is the Reed Gold Mine. This was the location of the first significant gold discovery in the United States. In 1799, a young Conrad Reed discovered a shiny yellow rock in a nearby creek one Sunday afternoon weighing seventeen pounds. Not knowing what it was, it served as a doorstop for three years before it was sold for $3.50 to a merchant. John Reed, Conrad's father, began to mine the area for more of the precious metal. In a relatively short time frame, the area became the home of America's first gold rush. It was significant enough that the United States government established a Mint in nearby Charlotte, North Carolina, to produce coinage from the gold.

Bill Johnson, the former pastor of Bethel Church in Redding, California, points out that gold is hidden in the ground because only the diligent will dig it out. We qualify ourselves for the benefits of a particular revelation by digging out its truths. The concept of the Courts of Heaven is one such truth.

In the story of Reed's gold discovery, although the young boy did not have to dig for the gold to discover it, he did not know what he had, so it only served as a doorstop. It was not until later that its value began to be understood.

Some have wanted to find a long treatise in the Word that would just "lay it out," but may I remind the reader that some beliefs we hold dear have less scriptural backing than the Courts of Heaven concept possesses. As charismatics we value the idea of the Baptism in the Holy Spirit; however, to come to embrace such a concept requires a snippet of scripture here and a piece in another place. It is not so neatly laid out as we would like. The fact that it is not neatly laid out does not diminish its value or truth; it simply requires a bit of diligence to study it out and embrace it. Many other doctrines are the same way (i.e. the Trinity, healing, and more).

Over the course of this introduction to the concept of the Courts of Heaven, I will only identify and begin laying the foundation for it. As you read, have enough openness of mind to recognize that just because you never saw it in scripture does not mean it was not in scripture. When introduced to something unfamiliar, it is natural that we have our defenses up. However, I ask that as you review this material, you consider "What if?" What if it is true? What if it is entirely valid? What if it is a concept that has viability for the times we live in? Is it possible that this understanding is just now coming to light because we need more powerful tools in our belt to deal with the situations in which we find ourselves? I believe you will conclude that the concept is real, valid, and quite viable for the times in which we live. It is another tool in our belt.

Many of the things I initially learned were via Robert Henderson's CD series on *Navigating the Court System of Heaven*. I am grateful for Robert's ministry and for being a voice for this message. I hope that the concepts I teach will mesh well with his teaching. As that occurs, the body of Christ will gain strength and increase in strategy in this paradigm of prayer.

For the most part, I will be teaching in this book on successfully dismantling accusations that are arrayed against us. We find evidence in the Scriptures of several different courts, each serving a function in the Court System of Heaven. In this book, I will be dealing with one I call the Mercy Court, which some have termed the "Mobile Court." We are instructed in Hebrews 4:16:

> *Let us, therefore, come boldly to the throne of grace that we may obtain mercy and find grace to help in time of need.*

For instance, my great-grandfather had some hand tools that he used extensively. One was called a brace and bit. It was a hand-powered drill with which to make holes in wood. I have a similar tool now, but it is powered by electricity, known as a power drill. They both have the same result, but the electric drill is far more effective and efficient than the old brace and bit. So it is with prayer. We need tools that are even more effective than the older ones. They are still valid paradigms of prayer, but the Courts of Heaven touch on concepts more effectively and efficiently than I've seen in the other prayer models. In over forty years of ministry, I have done a lot of praying. Look at the Courts of Heaven concept as another tool in your tool belt. It does not need to replace other devices, but it has its place. Let's get the job done!

This brief booklet will help you understand one of the vital principles of the Mercy Court of Heaven. I encourage you to order the full book: *The Courts of Heaven: An Introduction.*

Many blessings,

Dr. Ron Horner

Chapter 1

The Purpose of Accusations

To understand the importance of the Mercy Court and how it can be utilized to impact our lives positively, we need to know one of its chief functions. In the Mercy Court, we deal with the dismantling of accusations that are arrayed against us.

An accusation is defined by dictionary.com as:

> *a charge of wrongdoing; imputation of guilt or blame.*[1]

That is a legal definition, but when we understand that the end goal of an accusation is to divert you from your purpose, we realize we can no longer ignore these allegations. Left unresolved, they will not simply go away. Rather, they will fester, causing more and

---

[1] "Accusation Definition & Meaning." Dictionary.com. Accessed August 26, 2016. http://www.dictionary.com/browse/accusation.

more grief in our lives and in the lives of those we love. Here is one pastor's story:

> *As pastor of my church, I was merely ignoring the accusations I was hearing. What I did not realize is that although they may not have been affecting me, they were affecting my church and my congregation. Since learning about the Courts of Heaven, I have begun to deal with the accusations and get them dismantled.*
>
> *Rev. Virgil Harris*
> *Calvary Redemption*
> *Center Church,*
> *Spartanburg, SC*

Purpose #1:
To divert you from your purpose

We know that our adversary is Satan. In the New Testament, the word 'Satan' is sometimes translated as 'accuser.' Therefore, it stands to reason that one of the chief functions of the adversary is to accuse.

Remember the story of Peter, who, when Jesus told him that he (Jesus) would die shortly, was sharply rebuked by Jesus.

> *But when He **(Jesus)** had turned around and looked at His disciples, He rebuked Peter, saying, "Get behind Me, Satan **(Accuser)**! For you are not mindful of the things of God, but the things of men." (Mark 8:33) (Emphasis mine)*

Was Jesus really calling Peter 'Satan?' No, he wasn't. He was saying, "Get behind me, you accuser, you want to divert me from my purpose. I must suffer and die. I must fulfill my purpose even if it is not what you envision."

Jesus identified the accusation and its intent—to divert him from his purpose. He recognized that Peter did not want Jesus to suffer and die. That was not his idea of a Messiah-King. Jesus, however, would NOT be diverted from his purpose—regardless of who was speaking.

Accusation:

An implication of wrong

or incapability designed

to hinder the fulfillment

of your purposes in God.

---

*Accusations that are taken
to heart alter destinies*

Purpose #2:
To deceive you

Accusations often come in the 'first person,' meaning they are designed to trick you into believing it is your personal thought. For example: "I can never do anything right!" We embrace that accusation and allow it to sap our strength. If it is allowed to go unchecked in our minds, we will start voicing the accusation, saying, "I can never do anything right." We may then find things begin to not go right. By embracing the lie, we empower the liar (who is Satan). Philippians 4:13 tells us,

> *I can do all things through Christ who strengthens me.*

Paul reminded us in Romans 8:1,

> *There is therefore now no condemnation to those who are in Christ Jesus, who do not walk according to the flesh, but according to the Spirit.*

A simple way to remember this is:

*The accuser accuses
while the Comforter comforts.*

As we dismantle these accusations and embrace the Father's and Jesus's viewpoint of us, freedom can come because we are embracing the truth. Remember...

And you shall know the truth, and the truth shall make you free. (John 8:32)

*If what it is saying
is contrary to the Word of God,
it is an accusation, and therefore,
it did not find its origin in Heaven!*

Purpose #3:
To discourage you

We must keep in mind that the intent of the adversary in incessantly badgering you with accusations is to wear you out.

Accusations MUST be answered!

Remember, he will sap your strength, then plunder your palaces.[2] He seeks to divert you from your purpose because he fears you fulfilling your purpose. He attempts to neutralize your impact and effect for the Kingdom of God.

Typical Accusations

People in General

Typical accusations people deal with can be these:

- I'm not worthy.
- I'm stupid.
- I'm selfish.
- I'm unattractive.
- I don't have anything to offer.
- I can't be forgiven.
- I can't do what God is asking.

Wives

Wives often deal with accusations such as these:

- My husband doesn't love me.

---

[2] Amos 3:11 Therefore, thus says the Lord GOD: "An adversary shall be all around the land; he shall sap your strength from you, and your palaces shall be plundered."

- My husband is an adulterer.
- My husband is an alcoholic.
- My husband is a drug addict.
- My husband is a wife beater.
- My husband is lazy.
- My husband is no good.
- My husband is a workaholic.
- My husband is a terrible father.
- My husband is a cheater.
- My husband is a liar.
- My husband is a terrible son to his parents.
- He's just like his father.
- He's a terrible parent to our children.
- I can't please my husband.
- I can never make him happy.

Husbands

Husbands often deal with these accusations:

- My wife doesn't love me.
- My wife is an adulterer.
- My wife is an alcoholic.
- My wife is a drug addict.
- My wife is abusive.
- My wife is lazy.
- My wife is no good.
- My wife is a workaholic.

- My wife is a terrible mother.
- My wife is a cheater.
- My wife is a liar.
- My wife is a terrible daughter to her parents.
- My wife can never make me happy.

Parents

Parents often hear these about their children:

- My son/daughter can't do anything right!
- My son/daughter doesn't love me.
- My son/daughter is an adulterer.
- My son/daughter is an alcoholic.
- My son/daughter is a drug addict.
- My son/daughter is a spouse beater.
- My son/daughter is lazy.
- My son/daughter is no good.
- My son/daughter is a workaholic.
- My son/daughter is a terrible father/mother.
- My son/daughter is a cheater.
- My son/daughter is a liar.
- My son/daughter is stupid.
- My son/daughter is a terrible son/daughter.

Children

Children, on the other hand, may hear accusations such as these:

- I can't do anything right!
- My father/mother doesn't love me.
- My father/mother is an adulterer.
- My father/mother is an alcoholic.
- My father/mother is a drug addict.
- My father/mother is a spouse beater.
- My father/mother thinks I'm lazy.
- I'm no good.
- I'll never measure up to mom's/dad's expectations.
- Life isn't worth living.
- I am a terrible son/daughter.
- I'm a bad student.

Singles

Singles, on the other hand, have different accusations they may deal with:

- What's wrong with me?
- Why can't I find a mate?
- I don't deserve a husband/wife.
- I'll never get married.

About Others

We even make accusations about others that are having an impact:

- They are a thief.
- They are an adulterer.
- They are no good.
- They are a worthless bum.
- They are a sinner.
- They are a drunk.
- They are a drug addict.
- They are a greedy person.
- They are a selfish person.
- They are a gossiper.
- They are a liar.
- They are a lazy person.
- They are a racist.
- They are a control freak.
- They are abusive.
- They are a Jezebel.
- They are self-centered.

Now that you've seen some of the accusations people deal with, can you see how embracing any of these can hinder you from fulfilling your destiny? It is crucial that we learn to identify these accusations and get them dismantled so we can stop their impact on our lives and the lives of others.

If you, as a parent, were to say in frustration, "My child is simply no good!" Imagine you are now in a court of law, and the accuser is taking those words (that you spoke out of frustration) and speaking to the court. He may say, "Your honor, even her parents say he/she is no good!" We have given him ammunition against them in the Courts of Heaven.

That declaration becomes an accusation and is utilized by the adversary to impact the child's destiny.

The pattern is the same for all of us.

If you took any of the accusations listed on the prior pages and asked, 'How will this impact their destiny?' we might find ourselves much more cautious about the words that come out of our mouth—particularly those spoken in frustration. We must learn to guard our lips to avoid saying things we later regret. The words that come out of our mouths cannot be erased without legal action in the Courts of Heaven.

Testimonies

Following one of your seminars, in our session, we took my grandson who was experiencing a great deal of anger to the Mercy Court. He would explode in anger and throw things. His parents did not know what to do. After dealing with the accusations against him, the anger ceased. He is now the top of his class in school.

A Thankful Grandmother

Another testimony from the same seminar:

We took my son to the Mercy Court. He had gotten involved with the wrong crowd and was involved in drugs. Part of our petition was that God would separate him from the bad influences. In a very short period of time, one of his drug friends had died tragically, two others were put in prison, and the third had to flee the area because of troubles with other drug dealers. My son showed up at the church one Sunday morning and walked to the front, surrendering his life to God. He is now involved in the church, writing songs, and growing in God. Hallelujah!

A Grateful Mom

Purpose #4:

To divide you

The agenda of any accusation is to divide and dominate. (2 Corinthians 2:11 MIRROR)

The first casualty of an accusation is to divide you from the truth. If a spouse makes an accusation against their spouse, the intent of that accusation is to divide those people. If a parent accuses their child, a divide will occur between the parties that will (if left unresolved) harm the relationship.

Purpose #5:

To dominate you

If left unresolved, an accusation can eventually dominate one's life and relationships. For example, if a couple accuses one of the parties' parents due to the divide that accusation created, the parties will then be dominated by the accusation, whether it is true or not.

When we recognize the purposes behind accusations, we are more likely to be careful about what we say about a person, a ministry, a business, or a government. Remember that in Luke 6:28, Jesus said to bless those who curse you and pray for those who despitefully use you. To despitefully use someone is to insult, slander, and falsely accuse them. Since the Golden Rule says to do to others as you would have them do unto you, when someone takes it upon themselves to accuse, slander, or insult you falsely, they are stepping in league with the accuser of the brethren. "Your safety in Me," Heaven said, "is that you walk in love one with one another."

When you enter accusation, you have stepped out of love and leaned toward hatred. You only have two choices: you either love someone or hate them. If you are actively not loving them, you may be demonstrating hatred toward them. That is not a safe place to be.

John the Apostle understood this. He wrote plainly in 1 John 3:8: He who sins is of the devil. In v. 15, he writes that he who hates his brother is a murderer. If you try to murder someone, either their character or their person, you have stepped out of love and into a place of hatred. Blessing cannot rest on that place.

Therefore, if it cannot land, it must return to the one that sent it. When it returns, it contains the same harvest which was originally sent. If it was a ten-fold harvest when sent, then it would be a ten-fold harvest when it lands upon the sender.[3]

---

[3] "Chapter 1: Return to Sender." In *Engaging Heaven for Revelation for Revelation – Volume 1*, 3. LifeSpring Publishing, 2020.

Purpose #6:
To defeat you

The accuser goes to bring accusations against us. Sometimes, the enemy comes to us personally, speaking to us—where to accuse ourselves, where we accuse others in our hearts and our minds.

It is not a sin until we embrace it and we act upon it.

Satan is always looking for openings with which to impact us negatively. When we make an accusation, we have essentially sided with Satan and have become an "accuser of the brethren." This can extend to what happens when we accuse ourselves of things. Maybe we messed up somewhere, and we said to ourselves, "I'm a terrible parent." We have, therefore, made an accusation about ourselves that the enemy will be glad to use against us. He can use it against us to disqualify us from something Heaven has for us, saying, "Your Honor, this person has been an accuser of the brethren. Therefore, you must deny their request." We have inadvertently given him ammunition and he is happy to use it against us to impact our lives negatively.

Purpose #7:
To delay you

If the enemy can keep you from progressing forward, he will. Often, we will inadvertently help him by embracing accusations that have been placed against us or agreeing with the accusations made by others against someone. The endgame for Satan is to hinder us from fulfilling our purpose upon the earth. Let's not help him with that.

In Luke 6:6-7, we read:

> *The law professors and Pharisees were watching him insidiously, to see whether he would heal on the Sabbath day. These typical plaintiffs, were hoping to gather more evidence in building their growing case of accusation against Jesus. (MIRROR)*

In this passage, the word "accusation" is shown to come from two Greek words, *kate* (downward) and *goros* (to trade), from which we get the word category. It means to trade downward. When we accuse someone, we are categorizing them in a negative fashion. We are essentially placing them in a category of some sort.

Purpose #8:
To defer hope

Whenever we are making requests in prayer, those are trades we are making with Heaven. Satan loves to hinder and interrupt those trades so that we do not receive what we desire and, therefore, experience hope deferred. The accuser will say that we could not have full access to Heaven for the trade because of generational sin and iniquity. However, we can ask Jesus to begin advocating on our behalf, saying that because of what He did on the cross, that gave the person free access to the trades and goods and services of Heaven.

Many times, the accuser can bring legal paperwork *against* the generational line, but there is also legal paperwork *for* the generational line.

Purpose #9:
To destroy your health

The need to deal with accusations against our health or well-being doesn't end with the Mercy Court which we will discuss shortly. Although we generally deal with them in the Mercy Court. Accusations must be dealt with in every arena.

Since one purpose of an accusation is to divert you from your purpose, if you are suffering from an affliction and *the accusation is that you will never get better,* if that accusation is embraced and not dismantled, you will not be able to fulfill your purpose.

A sickness itself is an accusation!

The purpose of sickness is to divert you from your purpose, and because of that, it must be dealt with. Follow the four-step process I teach to dismantle them in your life so you can move ahead. We will also discuss that shortly.

These simple steps have helped many come to freedom from the power the accusations were placed against their lives.

---

*Accusations place you
under pressure.*

Suppose the accusation is:

You brought this on yourself!

Don't argue the point! Simply agree with the adversary, confess it as sin, repent, and ask that the blood of Jesus be applied to the accusation and its ramifications.

We can waste a lot of time defending ourselves, but remember, if we are not personally guilty of the accusation, the chances are quite strong that someone in our lineage is guilty. Suppose you went shopping with someone, and while in the store, they decide to shoplift an item. You know nothing about it, but after they shoplift the item, they place it in your purse, bag, or pocket and leave the store.

As you leave the store, you are apprehended, and the item is found in your possession. The store's management may not be very interested in hearing that you did not shoplift, only that you were caught with the item in your possession.

That is how Satan views our situation. Because every trauma or fear that our ancestors experienced is embedded in their DNA and, at our conception, is passed on to us and marked in our DNA, he considers us guilty. It's in our possession! We may not have committed the sin, but we carry evidence of the item within us.

Purpose #10:

To divide your family

In some cases, entire families are under the influence of accusations that are keeping the whole family from experiencing God's best for their lives regarding their health or welfare. In this situation, the father, mother (or both) can step into their role as priests and get the accusations dealt with. Deal with *every* accusation.

What if the accusation is that we were disobedient? The answer is simple: Repent! Receive forgiveness and move ahead. We all have messed up at some point in time. Just because you have a flat tire, you don't stop driving, and you don't throw away the vehicle. Simply get the flat tire changed and be on your way!

Accusations affect your behavior,
but false verdicts
dictate your behavior.

Deal with familial accusations just as you would with personal accusations. Use the guidelines in this book to take care of them.

Purpose #11:
To disparage your ministry and message

*²² Then one was brought to Him **who was demon-possessed** (demonized), blind and mute; and He healed him, so that the blind and mute man both spoke and saw. ²³ And all the multitudes were amazed and said, "Could this* *be the Son of David?" (Matthew 12:22-23) (Emphasis mine & additions mine)*

The multitudes had not seen ministry on this scale by anyone up to that time.

Immediately, Jesus is accused of casting out demons by the prince of demons.

^{24} Now when the Pharisees heard it they said, "This fellow does not cast out demons except by Beelzebub, the ruler of the demons." ^{25} But Jesus knew their thoughts, and said to them: "Every kingdom divided against itself is brought to desolation, and every city or house divided against itself will not stand. ^{26} If Satan casts out Satan, he is divided against himself. How then will his kingdom stand? ^{27} And if I cast out demons by Beelzebub, by whom do your sons cast them out? Therefore, they shall be your judges. ^{28} But if I cast out demons by the Spirit of God, surely the kingdom of God has come upon you. ^{29} Or how can one enter a strong man's house and plunder his goods, unless he first binds the strong man? And then he will plunder his house. (Matthew 12:24-29)

One attack against us is to attack our message or our ministry. Attacks can taint others' perceptions of us and need to be dismantled. Remember, accusations stand until dealt with.

Purpose #12:

To devour your stuff

Amos, the Old Testament prophet, had this to say about our adversary:

Therefore thus says the Lord GOD: "An adversary shall be all around the land; He shall sap your strength from you, And your palaces shall be plundered." (Amos 3:11)

If the enemy, through discouragement, can sap your strength, he will have little trouble plundering your palaces. He can access your stuff because you don't have the energy to fight and withstand him.

Get the accusations resolved so they no longer restrain you from the Father's best for your life.

Chapter 2
Accusations Reveal Strategy

One positive aspect of an accusation is that it reveals Satan's strategy against us. If we can identify the accusation, we can uncover the strategy. If we know the strategy, we can learn to counter it with Heaven's insight.

---

*Learning to recognize
an accusation is vital.*

Here are some key points about accusations:

- Accusations often hide behind innuendo and subtleties;
- Accusations are thoughts that are not generally edifying;

- Accusations start in the mind as a simple thought that often does not have much emotion associated with it;
- Accusations often come as simple ideas into our minds;
- Accusations give us (or others) an altered perspective of us (or others);
- Accusations can give an altered perspective of things in our lives or even another gospel altogether;
- Accusations may be veiled in flattery;
- Accusations, when embraced, can bear the wrong fruit in our lives;
- Accusations are often a perversion of a promise of God.

As we realize that the accuser plants these thoughts to access our lives, we can gain the upper hand. The accuser wants us to believe that these ideas are ours so that we will follow them. However, we always have the ability to choose.

If an accusation is brought
and no answer is given
to the charge,
it stands as a fact
whether it is or not.

Job experienced this when he failed to provide a defense in court in both Job 1 and Job 2. The devil objects to the will of God through our personal sins, motives, or unforgiveness in our hearts. Other factors may come into play, but these are common ones.

Robert Henderson, who often teaches on the Courts of Heaven, put it this way:

> *Every accusation, whether made by people, heard in your mind, or directly by Satan or his forces, is an exposure of what Satan is using against you in the Courts of Heaven! The enemy will use the accusations of men in the Courts of Heaven against you.[4] Satan is not the only one talking junk about you. Often, the words of men will reveal the enemy's strategy against you. If you listen to the accusations of others: parents, children, friends, pastors, teachers, neighbors, or co-workers; you may discern the particular tactic at work at the present time.*

You may have experienced an onslaught of people accusing you of something. Sudden attacks are evident revelations of the nature of the assault. Determine what is being said, and if it is the same underlying

---

[4] Robert Henderson, *Navigating the Court System of Heaven*, DVD. www.roberthenderson.org

message, then that is the strategy being used against you in the courts.

Chapter 3

Dismantling the Accusations

We do not have to live as victims of the charges against us. Jesus gave us a strategy for dealing with them. However, the way to deal with them requires something we often do not want to provide—humility.

Agreeing with Your Adversary

As we read Matthew 5, you will see what I mean. I will quote the passage in context:

> *^{22} But I say to you that whoever is angry with his brother without a cause shall be in danger of the judgment. And whoever says to his brother, 'Raca!' shall be in danger of the council. But whoever says, 'You fool!' shall be in danger of hell fire. ^{23} Therefore if you bring your gift to the altar, and there remember that*

your brother has something against you, ²⁴ leave your gift there before the altar, and go your way. First, be reconciled to your brother, and then come and offer your gift. ²⁵ **Agree with your adversary quickly, while you are on the way with him,** *lest your adversary deliver you to the judge, the judge hand you over to the officer, and you be thrown into prison. ²⁶ Assuredly, I say to you, you will by no means get out of there till you have paid the last penny. (Matthew 5:22-26) (Emphasis mine)*

This passage is speaking within the confines of a court. Jesus is speaking, and his instruction to us is clear:

Agree with your adversary quickly...

We often want to say, 'NO!' I won't agree because I'm not guilty. Jesus, in this passage, is not implying guilt or innocence. That is not even part of the picture. He only said to agree with the adversary.

Why would you want to do that? Let me give you a few reasons:

1) **Jesus instructed us to.** That is reason enough.
2) **It stops the argument.** If someone wants to debate with you, yet you refuse to discuss in return, it ceases the argument. Your opponent is expecting you to rare up and start fighting.

3) **It puts you in position for the Lord to fight your battles.** Paul reminds us in Romans 12:19 "Beloved, **do not avenge yourselves**, but rather give place to wrath; for it is written, 'VENGEANCE IS MINE, I WILL REPAY,' says the Lord." We are explicitly instructed to not avenge ourselves. My guilt or innocence is not in question. Am I going to be obedient to the Lord and obey his instruction here?
4) **I may not be guilty, but if one of my ancestors was guilty, then it is in my DNA.** I may not be guilty of the actual sin, but I do have a responsibility to deal with the resulting curse. If my repentance on behalf of the particular deed will stop the advancement of that curse to future generations, then I should do so. **It won't matter if I did it because I am getting it under the blood of Jesus!** We will discuss this more in a moment because whether or not I did, it will quickly become a moot point.

Other reasons exist, but these are the primary reasons.

People's reasons for not following this first step generally boil down to one simple thing: pride. We must ask ourselves, 'Did we really EVER not do the deed in question?' Would we have done it if no one was watching? What have our ancestors done that, although we are not guilty of their sin, we have inherited some of the grief they caused?

Jeremiah spoke very plainly in Jeremiah 17:9 when he said:

> *The heart is deceitful above all things and desperately wicked: who can know it?*

A simple four-step process is what I utilize in getting these accusations dismantled. Let's look at what they are:

1) Agree with the adversary,
2) Confess it as sin,
3) Repent,
4) Apply the blood of Jesus.

I'll discuss this in more detail in a few moments, but I want to reiterate that it really doesn't matter if I did it or not. Within a few moments, the issue will be covered in the blood of Jesus, so it won't matter.

I've had people try to refute the sin by claiming that they did not commit the sin, but Jesus did not say to refute it. He said only, 'Agree with the adversary.' The agreement begins the process of dismantling the accusation.

Others try to apply Colossians 2:13-15:

> *And you, being dead in your trespasses and the uncircumcision of your flesh, He has made alive together with Him, having forgiven you all trespasses, [14] having wiped out the handwriting of requirements that was against*

> us, which was contrary to us. And He has taken it out of the way, having nailed it to the cross. ¹⁵ Having disarmed principalities and powers, He made a public spectacle of them, triumphing over them in it.

However, this passage must be taken in its context. We must remember when interpreting the Bible that *Scripture can never mean what it never would have meant to those to whom it was written.* We must keep this principle in mind. To do otherwise opens the door for all types of wrong interpretations.

This passage refers to Jesus successfully doing away with the requirements of the old Jewish code concerning sins. Jesus, when he gave his life and through the shedding of his blood on the cross, successfully abolished the old covenant requirements. Before the crucifixion, the sins of the people were defined and held against them. It required the blood of bulls, sheep, or other animals to have them blotted out. Jesus, by his death on the cross, blotted them out once and for all. The particular context of this verse deals with the erasure of sins via the blood of Jesus. The book of Hebrews explains in detail this truth. It was not and is not referring to the same accusations referring to the same accusations I have been speaking of. What I refer to are the charges, which are everyday things you and I have had to contend with. It does not impact our salvation, but it may impact our way of life.

Another passage people want to pull out can be found in Revelation 12:10:

> *¹⁰ Then I heard a loud voice saying in Heaven, "Now salvation, and strength, and the kingdom of our God and the power of His Christ have come, **for the accuser of our brethren, who accused them before our God day and night, has been cast down.***

However, it is rarely quoted in context, which is as follows:

> *⁹ So the great dragon was cast out, that serpent of old, called the Devil and Satan, who deceives the whole world; he was cast to the earth, and his angels were cast out with him. ¹⁰ Then I heard a loud voice saying in Heaven, "Now salvation, and strength, and the kingdom of our God and the power of His Christ have come, for the accuser of our brethren, who accused them before our God day and night, has been cast down. ¹¹ And they overcame him by the blood of the Lamb and by the word of their testimony, and they did not love their lives to the death.*

Part of the trouble with Revelation is determining if the verse being read is in the past, present, or future. I believe they are primarily past tense. However, many of the truths of the Word may be present facts but not actualized in our lives. The truth is, Satan is the accuser of the brethren, and I'm one of the brethren. I know I have been accused and want it successfully dealt with.

I knew of a young man who, although brilliant, had some holes in his belief system. He believed that if he did not believe a demon could affect him, it could not. Judging from his life, where he walked away from pursuing God and got involved in drugs and illicit sex, as well as other things, demons may have been affecting him much more than he realized. I do not have to believe that lightning can hurt me for it to happen. Some things don't require our belief for them to be realities.

A third passage that has been used comes from Isaiah 54:17. It is a wonderful promise but is misapplied when dealing with accusations. Let's look at it:

> *No weapon formed against you shall prosper, and every tongue which rises against you in judgment you shall condemn. This is the heritage of the servants of the LORD, and their righteousness is from Me," Says the LORD. (Isaiah 54:17)*

The key to understanding what we have the right to refute is the phrase 'against you in judgment.' Accusations have not made it to the point of judgment unless you have not shown up for court. If you have not shown up for court, the accuser may have received a default judgment against you. To receive a just judgment in your favor, you must be present in court and deal successfully with the accusations using the principles in this book and in my book *Overcoming Verdicts from the Courts of Hell*.[5] I will discuss this further a bit later.

Now, back to the four keys to dismantling accusations:

Step 1:
Agree with the adversary

Remember, it is easier to agree and trust God for vindication than to try to vindicate yourself.

We have discussed this fairly thoroughly, so let's proceed.

Step 2:
Confess it as Sin

John, the beloved apostle, wrote in 1 John 1,

> *[8] If we say that we have no sin, we deceive ourselves, and the truth is not in us. [9] If we confess our sins, He is faithful and just to*

---

[5] Available at www.ronhorner.com.

forgive us our sins and to cleanse us from all unrighteousness. ¹⁰ If we say that we have not sinned, we make Him a liar, and His word is not in us. (1 John 1:8-10)

The word confess implies that we are to say the same thing that God says about our sins. It is an acknowledgment that the deed was, in fact, a sin before God. And if we had done the deed, it would have been a sin. People are often not sorry for their sins; they are merely sorry they got caught in it. In the context of the passage, John is letting us know that to think we never, ever did a thing or never would is a deception. To believe that we have never sinned is to make God out as a liar (v. 10).

Proverbs 28:13 reminds us:

He who covers his sins will not prosper, but whoever confesses and forsakes them will have mercy.

I want mercy. How about you?

Imagine this scenario:

You are driving along when suddenly you notice in your rearview mirror the flashing lights of a highway patrolman or policeman. You glance at the odometer and realize you have been speeding. At that moment, are you praying for justice or mercy? I doubt many of us are praying, 'O please God, let him give me a ticket!'

No, we are praying for mercy.

Now, on to step 3...

Step 3:

Repent

As believers, we should live in a repentant mode. I heard the late Bible teacher Kenneth E. Hagin gave some very sage advice when he said,

We should be quick to repent, quick to forgive, and quick to obey.

Living a repentant lifestyle helps us stay in tune with Holy Spirit. The word repent simply means:

...to turn back from, to change the mind concerning. It is acknowledgment plus action.

We are familiar with 2 Chronicles 7:14,

...if My people who are called by My name will humble themselves, and pray and seek My face, and __turn__ (repent) from their wicked ways, then I will hear from Heaven and will forgive their sin and heal their land. (Emphasis mine)

Isaiah enjoins us to...

*⁶ Seek the LORD while He may be found, Call upon Him while He is near. ⁷ Let the wicked forsake his way, And the unrighteous man his thoughts; Let him **return** to the LORD, And He will have mercy on him; And to our God, For He will abundantly pardon. (Isaiah 55:6-7) (Emphasis mine)*

While Ezekiel reminds us...

"Therefore I will judge you, O house of Israel, everyone according to his ways," says the Lord GOD. "Repent, and turn from all your transgressions, so that iniquity will not be your ruin." (Ezekiel 18:30)

Again, in a passage familiar to most of us, Isaiah points out...

But in that coming day, no weapon turned against you will succeed. You will silence every voice raised up to accuse you. These benefits are enjoyed by the servants of the LORD; their vindication will come from Me. I, the LORD, have spoken! (Isaiah 54:17 NLT)

I like how the God's Word translation voices it:

*"No weapon that has been made to be used against you will succeed. **You will have an answer for anyone who accuses you.** This is the inheritance of the LORD'S servants.*

Their victory comes from me," declares the LORD. (Isaiah 54:17 GW) (Emphasis mine)

What is that answer? Repentance!

Several translations have assumed that we do the condemning, but since we are not the judge, it is typically the responsibility of the judge in a courtroom to determine justification or condemnation. That is why I see it as allowing the Lord to vindicate and bring justice (a courtroom term) and allow him to do his job.

Step 4:

Apply the Blood

At this stage, we simply ask that the blood of Jesus be applied to the sin and to every ramification of that sin. Why do I state it that way? Because when a sin is committed, it never impacts just one person. Others are always impacted. Take a situation where one of the married partners commits adultery. That adultery affects the offended spouse, and if the other adulterous partner is married, it affects their spouse. It may impact children, business situations, and other family members. You may sin alone, but the consequences you share with others. Our sins have created massive ripples as when a stone is thrown into the water.

Because I have applied the blood of Jesus, it dismantles the accusation and the associated arguments that the accuser may have brought against you. Satan understands that the highest answer to the sin problem is the application of the blood of Jesus. Jesus is the perfect sacrifice for our sins. Satan has no argument against that blood. He has no defense against it. We now can step into a new level of freedom from that accusation.

The Process

Step 1	Step 2	Step 3	Step 4
1	2	3	4
AGREE with the adversary	**CONFESS** the accusation as sin	**REPENT** Turn from that pattern of sin	**APPLY** the blood of Jesus to the sin
Matthew 5:28-29	1 John 1:9	2 Chronicles 7:14	1 John 1:7, 9

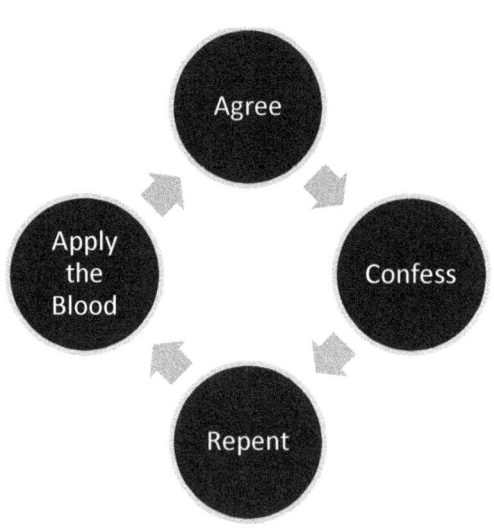

Chapter 4

The Mercy Court QuickGuide

Having taught dozens of seminars on the Mercy Court, it was apparent from the very beginning that people needed to be able to implement what I was teaching. Over the course of time, I have refined this QuickGuide for the purpose of doing just that. I have templates available in Word.docx format that can be downloaded so you can "fill in the blank," so to speak. It has never been my intent that these QuickGuides become "mechanical." When using them, we must be flexible and listen to the Father, Jesus, Holy Spirit and the Seven Spirits of God, as well as any others who may be permitted to speak.

As you follow along with this QuickGuide, you will get a feel for the typical procedure. I, as well as others, have used this QuickGuide hundreds of times and have seen lives changed through this paradigm of prayer.

While going through the QuickGuide, you may realize that you need more information. All you have to do is ask the court for a recess. It is like the Pause button on your DVD player. It pauses everything until you are able to return to the case. At which point, you will just resume the case. The fact that we are able to come back to the court was something the widow woman in Luke 18 understood. She was intent on returning as often as necessary. Using the pause in the Mercy Court seems to suspend whatever is going on. The enemy is restricted from doing further damage and must wait until the Court is back in session.

Let me reiterate. The QuickGuide is to help you along. It is not to become a formal, mechanical approach to dealing with accusations. If your heart is not right when you go into the Mercy Court, do not expect to have positive results. Our Father, the Just Judge, wants to see lives restored. He has unveiled this new tool so we can become more efficient in working with Him to bring people to freedom.

Mercy Court QuickGuide

[This QuickGuide follows the Mercy Court Process Chart available from www.ronhorner.com.]

[You or the party for whom you are going to Court is the Defendant.]

DEFENDANT: Father God, our Just Judge, I ask to enter the Courts of Heaven today.

I ask that Jesus Christ open all books on my behalf during this court session. May all records be reviewed and judged, and Court rulings manifested on earth.

I address this Court through the blood of Jesus and in the righteousness of Jesus. I ask through Jesus, my Advocate, that all Court parties be present. Included are the accuser of the brethren, the great cloud of witnesses who have testimony on my behalf, and the angelic hosts working for the Just Judge to enact His judgments, and the Seven Spirits of God and all other pertinent parties.

Presentation of Accusations

DEFENDANT: Today, I bring to Your Honor, through my Mediator, Jesus Christ, the following list of charges made against (me/defendant) by myself, others, and the workers of darkness.

[Present each accusation individually if possible.]

DEFENDANT: Your Honor, I present the accusation that "_____."

COURT: How do you plead?

DEFENDANT: I plead guilty, Your Honor, and according to Matthew 5:25-26, I agree with my adversary, and I confess this as sin. I repent of this sin and ask that the blood of Jesus be applied to this sin and all the ramifications of it, in Jesus' name.

I ask forgiveness for any action or reaction that caused this accusation to be made by (me/others), and I ask that it and all its ramifications be cleansed by the blood of Jesus.

Based on John 20:23, I choose to forgive (name of parties making the accusation) for their judgments against me, and I ask Our Father, the Just Judge, to forgive them.

I choose to forgive (the Defendant, if not yourself) of their sin in this matter and ask you to forgive it as well, Your Honor.

[Repeat this process for each accusation.]

Your Honor, I wish to repent for those things I have spoken against (myself/the Defendant) and ask your forgiveness of these words spoken, in Jesus' name. I ask that the blood of Jesus be applied to this sin and that it would be entirely erased from existence.

Calling of Witnesses

DEFENDANT: Your Honor, we would request that those who have testimony on (my/the Defendants') behalf be called to testify at this time.

[At this point, have the seers with you begin to listen and see who has presented themselves. Have these give their testimony. The Great Cloud of Witnesses may step up and provide further support of your faith in Jesus and walk with God. The Holy Spirit may even call forth a saint interceding on your behalf. You may even call Jesus to testify on your behalf.]

Submission of Testimony

DEFENDANT: Your Honor, at this time, I would like to present the following promises from the Word of God concerning this Defendant:

[Recite particular pertinent promises from the Word of God at this time.]

DEFENDANT: Your Honor, I would also like to present the following as testimony on <u>(the Defendants')</u> behalf.

[Recite/read prophetic words given concerning the Defendant.]

Closing Statement

DEFENDANT: Your Honor, we would request of the court the following:

[In the closing statement provide your suggested recourse if there has been an injustice made against you

(financial, relationship, etc. to be restored, perpetrators to be saved, etc.).]

DEFENDANT: I also ask the Courts regarding all accusations made against (the Defendant) by the accuser of the brethren to be stricken/purged from all records (Heaven and Hell, and with all reference to these accusations) that I have petitioned today in the blood of Jesus.

[Once you have received the verdict, you may then exit the Mercy Court to go to the next step.]

Closing Actions

[Enter the Court of Scribes]

DEFENDANT: We request permission to enter the Court of Scribes.

[Take a step into the Court of Scribes}

I request a copy of the verdict just handed down in my case.

[Receive the verdict from the court (perform the prophetic act of receiving the scroll or papers).]

[Once you have received it, thank the court and exit to enter the Court of Angels.]

DEFENDANT: I request permission to enter the Court of Angels.

[Step by faith, into the Court of Angels with your scroll.] (See Chapter 16.)

DEFENDANT: I have scrolls just issued from the courts, and I request angelic assistance to take care of these items.

[You will likely sense an angel or angels come forth (it may be one or many) and begin to take the scroll/papers from you. Once they are finished release them to go forth and take care of the verdict.]

[Now thank the court and exit.]

[You may rejoice now that your case has been heard and a decision rendered on your behalf. Some choose to take communion at this time.]

[At times, the judge will hand the paperwork directly to the bailiff, at which point your task is complete. Celebrate what the Lord has done on your behalf.

Common Questions

One of the most common questions I deal with is along these lines:

Question: We've gone to court, but I did something and interfered. Did that invalidate everything that was done in the courts?

Answer: Let's illustrate the answer this way. Suppose someone were to go to trial, get convicted, and be sentenced to prison. While being transported to the prison, the deputy made a mistake and the prisoner escaped. Would that invalidate what happened in the courts? No. The sheriff would go after the person, recapture them, and take them to prison. It is similar when dealing with the Courts of Heaven. When the court renders a verdict, the verdict stays rendered. The toughest part for some of us is to stay out of the way and let God work in the situation. He will take care of it. The Court System of Heaven is not so fragile that our mistakes can invalidate something God did. It is not like we can do something, and God and Jesus are sitting in Heaven with one of them saying, "I didn't see that coming. What are we going to do now?" No. God is not undone by our mistakes. He is not that fragile, and neither is the Court System of Heaven.

Question: Do we always go to the Court of Scribes and to the Court of Angels after a verdict is rendered?

Answer: Most of the time, yes. However, I have had many cases where the judge simply handed the paperwork/scrolls directly to the bailiff, and the bailiff took the verdict to the angels for dispatch. I have not discerned any hard and fast rule about it. It seems to be totally up to the judge. If the judge hands the verdict to the bailiff and does not engage you, do not be disappointed; he is simply making the most direct route for its' disposition. Receive the verdict in your heart and rejoice that the Just Judge ruled in your case.

Question: Do we always take Communion at the end of a court case?

Answer: My recommendation is you follow the leading of Holy Spirit. If directed to -- do. If not, don't. I do express my gratitude to the court whenever possible for hearing the case.

Question: Can I go to the Mercy Court for someone else?

Answer: Of course! You may present a case for anyone you feel led by the Holy Spirit to do so. Think of the freedom that can be brought to others as we dismantle the accusations working against their lives.

A printable version is available at www.ronhorner.com.

MERCY COURT PROCESS

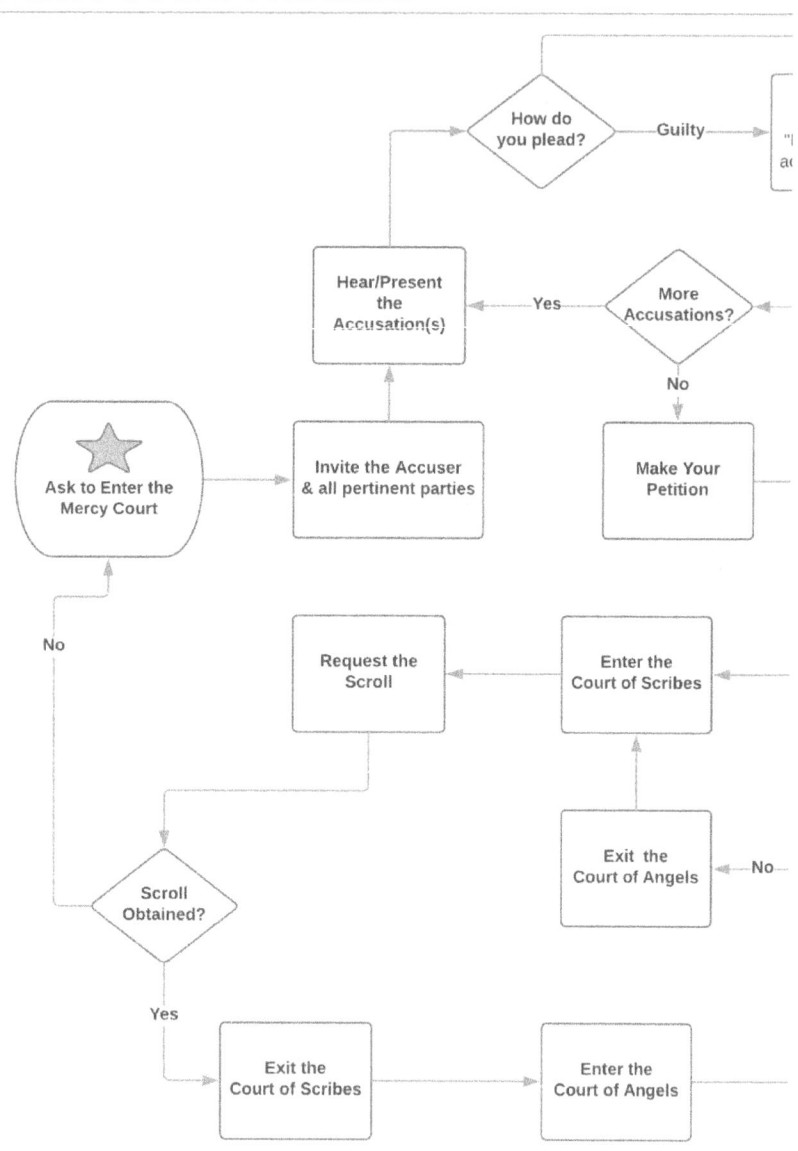

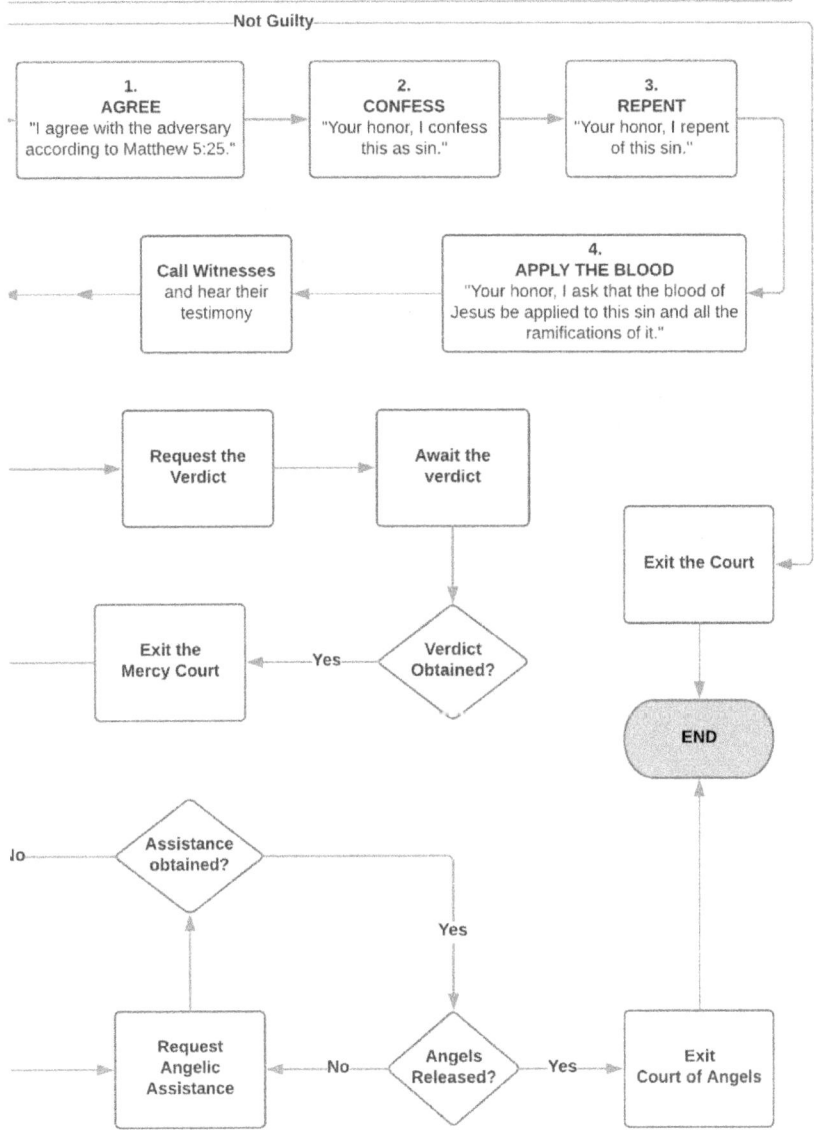

Chapter 5

Accusations Against Spiritual Sight

The need to deal with accusations against us doesn't end with the Mercy Court. Accusations against our sight must be dismantled in every arena. The purpose of an accusation is to divert you from your purpose. If you cannot see spiritually, and the accusation is that you will never be able to see, if that accusation is embraced and not dismantled, you will not be able to fulfill your purpose.

Sample Accusations

- You have no right to see!
- You are too young to see angels.
- You aren't spiritual enough to see.
- If you do that, you'll start seeing demons and junk!

Follow the four-step process I espouse to get accusations dismantled in your life so you can move ahead.

The Four Steps

1. Agree with the adversary (Matthew 5:25-26),
2. Confess it as sin (1 John 1:9),
3. Repent (Proverbs 28:13),
4. Apply the Blood of Jesus (1 John 1:7).

These simple steps have helped many enter freedom from the power the accusations were placed against their lives, no matter what the accusation was.

In some cases, entire families are under the pressure of accusations that are keeping the whole family from experiencing God's best for their lives regarding their health. In this situation, the father, mother (or both) can step into their role as priests and deal with the accusations. Deal with *every* accusation.

Recovering Sight[6]

1. Request access to the Court of Cancellations once you have dealt with the accusations,[7]

---

[6] For more on this, see my book *Unlocking Spiritual Seeing*, LifeSpring Publishing, 2019. Available at ronhorner.com.

[7] Accusations are generally dealt with in the Mercy Court but may be dealt with outside of any court; simply present testimony

2. Repent for embracing any lie that has affected your ability to see in the spirit,
3. Ask for forgiveness,
4. Forgive those making the accusations,
5. Bless them,
6. Release them,
7. Request restoration of your sight,
8. Request any covering over your sight be removed,
9. Begin to see!

---

of the fact you have dealt with the accusations in whatever court you are involved in.

Chapter 6
The Weapon of Blue Capture Bags

In a series of engagements with Heaven, we learned about a weapon that was described to us as capture bags. Many colors and purposes exist for these weapons, but one in particular helps us deal with accusations. We had seen blue capture bags but had no understanding of them. The blue bags capture the enemy's weapons.

Satan is a legalist, but he is also a copycat. His falsehood represents weaponry, as we would in the natural think of weaponry, but his weapons *are only tactics*. This has perplexed us in that, in the natural, we think of him attacking us with weapons. His weapons are *words* and *lies—tactical strategies of deception*. The blue bags capture the paradigms that perplex us.

When it comes to the enemy's warfare and talking about arrows, your armor will deflect the arrows from the enemy. We may have always assumed they were actual weapons. We saw them as actual arrows, but words or strategies can inflict more damage than a natural arrow ever could upon a person's realms.

We must have our angels capture the accusations!

In this paradigm, you don't have to get caught up in saying, 'Angels, go and capture the words and the phrases and the strategies.' Sending a blue bag will capture all of that and more. You can also say, 'Capture the accusations.' You can do that before the enemy has a legal right to bring it to the Courts of Heaven against you. This is the sovereignty of God on behalf of His sons.

Picture Jacob's ladder and how the accuser ascends and descends a ladder to bring accusations against us. Sometimes, the enemy comes to us personally, speaking to us about where to accuse ourselves or about where we accuse others in our hearts and our minds.

*To make an accusation
is not a sin until we embrace it
and we act upon it.*

This can be done to prevent those words and accusations of the enemy from reaching our spirit, and our heart, and our soul. Our repentance is for the entertaining of these accusations against others and against ourselves, et cetera. Before the enemy can take an accusation to the Courts of Heaven to accuse you where, you must come into agreement with the accuser; *the step before that* is when you come into agreement—you hear it, and you take it on. That is when he can have a legal right to accuse you.

*The blue capture bags are a part
of the paradigms of prayer
to forfeit the enemy's legal right
to form accusations against us.*

This is a gift from the Father. This bag is for His sovereignty towards us, in that if we can utilize this commissioning of the angels, it is a prevention of the next step of the enemy against us, which is where we would come into agreement or take on the accusation. It circumvents that for us *because we are His children*.

The Father is the one who has simplified this aspect, so we are not dealing with accusations over and over repeatedly. Heaven is simply taking that out of the equation for us. Look how the Father loves. That is what this is. He is giving you this tool. It's like a preventative medicine.

It is for dismantling something before it begins. It's a preventative.

People have just been sick and tired of the same accusations repeatedly. This tool is something we can use in our paradigms of prayer as we commission angels to use it on our behalf. We are not accepting or falling for the enemy's tactics but instead are being given Kingdom tactics that are offensive, not defensive. It is, for us, a preventative measure.

Chapter 7

Conclusion

As you exercise your faith and begin operating in the Courts of Heaven, you will find the promise of the Lord to respond speedily coming to pass in your life.

We will step into new levels of freedom as we use the Courts of Heaven paradigm to dismantle accusations that have been raised against us. Using the protocol taught in this book is a simple access point to engaging the Courts of Heaven, where you have the opportunity to change your life, the lives of your family, your church, your city, your state, and even your nation. Recent major events have been impacted by the actions of believers in the Courts of Heaven.

Believers across the globe are awakening to the potential within this paradigm of prayer. Courtroom prayer is changing lives, cities, and even the political landscape. As we become more well-versed in the operations of this court, we will see Jesus' command to disciple nations come to fulfillment. May we indeed disciple the nations!

Description

Accusations have great power to destroy your life and must be dealt with before they do. They create cases against you in the Courts of Heaven. The chief aim of an accusation is to divert your from your destiny. Accusations seek to define you and limit you and wear you down.

In this book, learn four simple keys to dismantling accusations against you and your family. This key to effectively fulfilling your purpose and cannot simply be ignored. Every accusation must be answered. They must be destroyed! Learn how in this book and step into new levels of freedom in your life!

About the Author

Dr. Ron Horner is an apostolic teacher specializing in the Courts of Heaven prayer paradigm. He has written over thirty books on the Courts of Heaven, engaging Heaven, working with angels, and living from revelation.

As founder of LifeSpring International Ministries, he currently trains people in engaging the Courts of Heaven in a weekly online teaching session. You can register to participate and discover more about the Courts of Heaven prayer paradigm on his various websites, classes, products, and services found here:

www.ronhorner.com

Other Books by Dr. Ron M. Horner

Building Your Business from Heaven Down

Building Your Business from Heaven Down 2.0

Building Your Business with the Blueprint of Heaven

Commissioning Angels – Volume 1

Cooperating with The Glory

Courts of Heaven Process Charts

Dealing with Trusts & Consequential Liens from the Courts of Heaven

Engaging Angels in the Realms of Heaven

Engaging Heaven for Revelation – Volume 1

Engaging Heaven for Revelation – Volume 2

Engaging Heaven for Trade

Engaging the Courts for Ownership & Order

Engaging the Courts for Your City (*Paperback, Leader's Guide & Workbook*)

Engaging the Courts of Healing & the Healing Garden

Engaging the Courts of Heaven

Engaging the Help Desk of the Courts of Heaven

Freedom from Mithraism

Kingdom Dynamics – Volume 1

Kingdom Dynamics – Volume 2

Let's Get it Right!

Lingering Human Spirits

Lingering Human Spirits – Volume 2

Living Spirit Forward

Next Dimension Access to the Court of Supplications

Overcoming the False Verdicts of Freemasonry

Overcoming Verdicts from the Courts of Hell

Releasing Bonds from the Courts of Heaven

The Courts of Heaven: An Introduction
(formerly *Engaging the Mercy Court of Heaven*)

The Four Keys to Dismantling Accusations – Second Edition

Unlocking Spiritual Seeing

Working with Your Realms & Your Realm Angels

SPANISH

Cómo Anular los Falsos Veredictos de la Masonería

Cómo Proceder en la Corte Celestial de Misericordia

Cómo Proceder en las Cortes para su Ciudad

Cómo Trabajar con Angeles en los Ambitos del Cielo

Cooperando con La Gloria de Dios

Las Cuatro Llaves para Anular las Acusaciones

Liberando Bonos en las Cortes Celestiales

Liberando Su Visión Espiritual

Sea Libre del Mitraísmo

Tablas de Proceso de la Cortes del Cielo

Viviendo desde el Espíritu

AFRIKAANS

Deelname aan Die Barmhartigheidshof van Die Hemel

Personal Advocacy Sessions

Do you feel like you need assistance?

We have several teams of trained advocates who assist our clients in resolving issues in the Courts of Heaven. Visit our website at **www.ronhorner.com** to find out more information.

www.ingramcontent.com/pod-product-compliance
Lightning Source LLC
Chambersburg PA
CBHW031414040426
42444CB00005B/559